WHAT IS YOUR CAT REALLY THINKING?

Copyright © Summersdale Publishers Ltd, 2016

Illustrations by Dannyboy

Text by Sophie Johnson

An Hachette UK Company
www.hachette.co.uk

Summersdale Publishers Ltd
Part of Octopus Publishing Group Limited
Carmelite House
50 Victoria Embankment
LONDON
EC4Y 0DZ
UK

www.summersdale.com

Printed and bound in the Czech Republic

ISBN: 978-1-84953-948-7

Substantial discounts on bulk quantities of Summersdale books are available to corporations, professional associations and other organisations. For details contact general enquiries: telephone: +44 (0) 1243 771107 or email: enquiries@summersdale.com.

# What Is Your
# Cat
# Really Thinking?

# What Is Your
# Cat
# Really Thinking?

WE NEED TO TALK ABOUT
YOUR CULINARY EFFORTS.

FELIX

Dannyboy
and Sophie Johnson

summersdale

YOU WORK TOO HARD.
WRITE A BLOG ABOUT HOW
CUTE I AM.

AH, SO YOU'RE AN ARIES! I KNEW IT!

I MADE AN ART.

WHERE'S ALL YOUR FUR? GROSS!
ARE YOU A SPHYNX OR SOMETHING?

BOX HUGS BETTER THAN YOU DO.
I LOVE BOX.

MEET MY NEW FRIENDS!
I CALL THE LITTLE ONE 'MR BITES'.

LOVELY. THREE MORE
THEN I'LL BITE YOU, THANKS.

CAT'S LOG, DAY 345. HUMAN FINALLY ACCEPTS HER PLACE IN THE HOME.

YOU SMELL GREAT TODAY.
NEW COLOGNE?

I'M SORRY, DID YOU THINK THIS WAS A TOKEN OF MY AFFECTION? IT ISN'T. IT'S A DEAD BIRD.

FEMALE HUMAN IS GONNA **LOVE** ME! THE DISTRESSED LOOK IS SO HOT RIGHT NOW.

YEAH, THIS GAME IS JUST GREAT.
NO, REALLY, HUMAN, YOU ARE SPOILING ME
WITH THIS PATHETIC BIT OF TAT.

EXCUSE ME, FOOD BRINGER,
YOU'RE SLEEPING THROUGH BREAKFAST.

YUCK! YOU DIDN'T EVEN
SNIFF HIS BUM YET!

DON'T LEAVE! HOW AM I SUPPOSED
TO IGNORE YOU if YOU'RE NOT HERE?

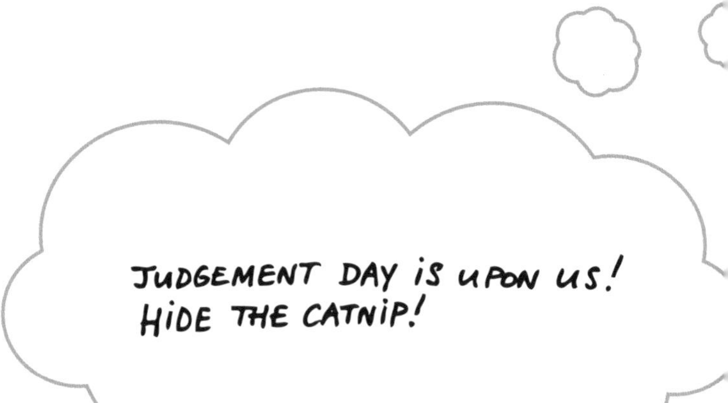
JUDGEMENT DAY IS UPON US!
HIDE THE CATNIP!

GOOD QUESTION. WHAT DO YOU
HAVE TO OFFER FOR EACH?

THREE ACROSS is 'INCANDESCENT.'
JEEZ, WHY DO YOU BOTHER?

NO, YOU'RE ADOPTED!

I SEE YOU WATCHING.
PERV.

THERE GOES THE NEIGHBOURHOOD.

I DON'T KNOW. I RECKON I COULD
TAME HIM WITH MY FELINE CHARMS.

WHO KEEPS PUTTING THIS TAT UP HERE?
THIS IS PRIME STRUTTING ESTATE.

I LET YOU DO THIS, I OWN THE HUMAN. DEAL

I GET NO REST
FROM THE PAPARAZZI.

SHE'S THE ONE I TOLD YOU ABOUT.
EATS HER OWN POOP.
DISGUSTING CREATURES.

YEAH? WELL MY BLOG'S GOT PHOTOS
OF YOU SNIFFING YOUR OWN PANTS.

Do you REALLY NEED ALL THIS STUFF
LYING AROUND? COME ON, DUDE,
HAVE SOME SELF-RESPECT.

SPOILER ALERT: IT TASTES BAD.
TAKE IT BACK AND GET SOMETHING
A LITTLE MORE CULTURED.

WELL, I WAS TAKEN FROM MY PARENTS AT
A YOUNG AGE. I DON'T THINK I EVER
FORGAVE THEM.

WELL I HOPE YOU KEPT THE RECEIPT?
THAT WAS RATHER A WASTED
EXPERIMENT IN FRUGALITY,
WASN'T IT?

YOGA IS GREAT FOR MY WELL-BEING.
I AM SO ZEN.

I WARNED YOU ABOUT FURBALLS.
CLASSY CATS DON'T SWALLOW.

FRUIT SNAKE!

If you're interested in finding out more about our books,
find us on Facebook at **Summersdale Publishers**
and follow us on Twitter at **@Summersdale**.

# www.summersdale.com